1991

W9-CZM-966

EcoZones

WETLANDS

Lynn M. Stone

Photos by Lynn M. Stone

ROURKE ENTERPRISES, INC.
Vero Beach, FL 32964

Library of Congress Cataloging in Publication Data

Stone, Lynn M.
    Wetlands / by Lynn M. Stone.
        p. cm. — (Ecozones)
    Includes index.
    Summary: Examines the wetland as an ecological niche and describes the plant and animal life supported there.
    ISBN 0-86592-447-3
    1. Wetland ecology — Juvenile literature.   2. Wetlands — Juvenile literature.   [1. Wetland ecology.   2. Ecology.]   I. Title.
II. Series: Stone, Lynn M.   Ecozones.
QH541.5.W3S76   1989
574.5'26325 — dc20   89-32742
                                                                        CIP
                                                                         AC

Contents

THE WETLANDS

Almost all of us, at one time or another, have boldly stepped into some place where the ground was mushy and the water oozed from our footprints. The bolder among us have squished and splashed deeper into this wetland environment, where our footprints immediately became secrets in the muck under a few inches of dark water. What lurked in that muddy, watery environment around our toes was hard to say. Still, we slogged on, carefully extracting each foot from the mire lest we plunge headlong into the water.

Whatever it was that beckoned some of us deep into the heart of a wetland was probably the same thing that kept other people far away. For every person who wants to see the wet haunts of water snakes, mink, moose, waterfowl, and strange, insect-eating plants, there are scores of people who prefer to keep dry, stable land underfoot and forego the firsthand view of nature.

The mix of water and mud and green plants that characterizes so many wetlands makes them foreboding for most people. But that mix of water and

Opposite *The Florida Everglades are a unique blend of marsh, swamp, river, and woodland.*

mud and green plants also makes wetlands one of the richest habitats on earth. The productivity of the wetlands, their cleansing ability, and their water storage capacity make them a resource to be highly cherished.

Wetlands defy a single or simple definition. They exist in many forms and in many locations. All of them share, however, a bond: they are places where the ground is wet or covered by shallow water. They are also dominated by plants that can live in wet or flooded conditions. In addition, wetlands have unique soils, different from dry, or upland, communities. Wetlands have several names, and each refers to a specific type of wetland **habitat**. They include bog, swamp, freshwater marsh, saltwater marsh, fen, **pocosin**, muskeg, and Everglades, to name a few.

In several places, wetlands are transitional habitats between solid ground and bodies of standing or flowing deep water, such as rivers, lakes, and oceans. The transitional nature of wetlands makes them difficult to define. It also contributes to one of their most appealing features—the diversity of life within them. Along with their store of wetland **organisms**, many wetlands also are part-time homes for life from both deep water and high ground. Many fish that spend their adult lives at sea spend their first days in the tidal waters of the salt marshes. Toads are quite at home in the forest's moist, leafy litter, but freshwater wetlands are critical for their reproduction. White-tail deer live near forest edges, but they often wade into marshes and swamps to browse.

Some kinds of wetlands—the Florida Everglades, for example—are unique to one location. Generally, any given kind of wetland can be found over a reasonably large area. Forested bogs, for instance, occur mostly in eastern Canada and the north central states, especially Minnesota. Bogs are usually found where the retreat of **glaciers** carved depressions in the earth. Freshwater marshes are scattered throughout the United States and the prairie provinces of Canada. Coastal saltwater marshes are found irregularly along the coasts of Canada and the United States. They are far more common along the Atlantic and Gulf of Mexico coasts than on the Pacific coast of the lower United States. They are also numerous in Alaska and in parts of Arctic Canada, particularly along the southern shore of Hudson Bay. Most of the various kinds of swamps are found in the eastern half of North America and in the Pacific Northwest.

Wetlands exist in exceedingly wide variety. Some are small and quite isolated, surrounded by forest, desert, or grassland. Others, like giant, shimmering saucers or leafy bowls, stretch for miles. No one knows just how much of North America is wetland. The figure varies, of course, with the definition and with changes caused by both man and climate. A recent estimate of wetland acreage in the United States, excluding Alaska and Hawaii, is 70 million.

TYPES OF WETLANDS

Many different forms of wetlands occur in North America. Each is not necessarily separate from another. In large wetland complexes, there are various types of wetlands overlapping and interacting with each other. Many swamps, for example, along the shores of rivers have marshy edges.

The most widely distributed wetlands are marshes. They are found in freshwater, saltwater, and **brackish** water environments. Brackish water is a blend of fresh and saltwater. Marshes are wetlands with large numbers of soft-stemmed plants. Many of these plants are **emergents**, plants that grow with their stems partly in and partly out of the water. Marshes are sunny, open wetlands because they have few, if any, trees.

Many freshwater marshes look like shallow, weedy ponds—with good reason. Ponds, as they age and fill with decaying vegetation, often become marshes. Freshwater marshes also develop along rivers or lakeshores.

Marshes can be relatively deep and have such aquatic plants as water lilies, pondweed, duckweed, and bladderwort. Some are seasonally dry, and others are little more than wet, seepy meadows.

Salt marshes are usually associated with ocean shores. These marshes are periodically flooded by tidal water. Salt marshes are typically populated by stands of cordgrass (*Spartina*) and black grass (*Juncus*), except in the Arctic. In the West, some inland marshes have salty water and plants associated with coastal salt marshes. These marshes, however, are unaffected by ocean tides.

Natural marshes are havens for wildlife, visible and invisible. Bright-as-

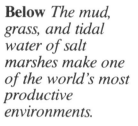

Below *The mud, grass, and tidal water of salt marshes make one of the world's most productive environments.*

new-paint dragonflies and damselflies zip from stem to stem. Ducks nest in the marsh edges and bob in the open water. Wakes trailing behind muskrats lead to domed lodges of cattails and other marsh plants.

One of the greatest concentrations of marshes in North America is in the prairie pothole country of south central Canada and the north central United States. Potholes are the handiwork of glaciers. They may be permanent sources of water, or they may dry up in late summer. Each spring melting snow and rain restores the dry potholes. They

Above *Marshes are wetlands with large numbers of soft-stemmed plants like the cattails shown in this Connecticut marsh.*

11

produce so many ducks that they are known as "duck factories."

Swamps are essentially marshes with trees or shrubs or a combination of the two. Some swamps, in fact, developed from marshes that filled with decaying vegetation and became drier over the years, making it possible for shrubs or trees to grow. Other swamps have developed along the shores of lakes or rivers. Some of America's greatest swamps lie in the backwaters or on the flood plains of rivers that periodically overflow their banks.

Swamps also emerge in poorly-drained lowlands, quite apart from any river or lake. Florida's magnificent Big Cypress Swamp is a great, shallow saucer that, for a large part of the year, retains water. Like other swamps, it supports water-loving trees, dominated by the bald cypress for which it was named.

Cypress swamps, found throughout the southeastern United States, are one of the most inviting wetlands. They are cool, green, and shadowy. By day they are haunted by the drumming of pileated woodpeckers and the flutter of startled wood ducks. By night they boom with the calls of barred owls and the grunting of alligators. Cypress

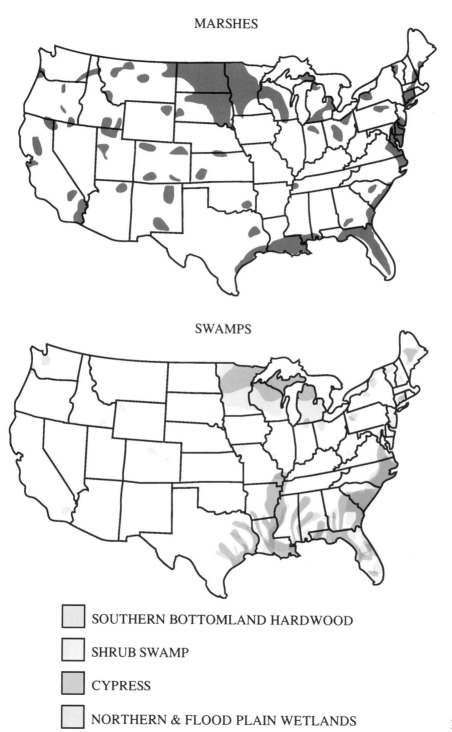

MARSHES

SWAMPS

SOUTHERN BOTTOMLAND HARDWOOD

SHRUB SWAMP

CYPRESS

NORTHERN & FLOOD PLAIN WETLANDS

13

"knees," projections of the cypress trees' root systems, poke up like snorkels. Long-legged wading birds, hunting for fish and snails, step gingerly into pools or probe the soft earth.

The National Audubon Society's Corkscrew Swamp Sanctuary in south Florida is one of the best examples of cypress swamp in the United States. A boardwalk snakes through a cypress forest of giant trees several hundred years old. Nearby is another remarkable swamp, the Fahkahatchee Strand. Its pop ash and pond apple trees, standing knee-deep in black water, are wrapped in leafy air-plants called **bromeliads** and epiphytic orchids. **Epiphytes** are plants that take their nourishment from air and rain rather than from soil.

Another type of swamp is the pocosin. Pocosins are found on the American coastal plain, from Virginia through the Carolinas. They are shrubby swamps with a scattering of trees. They are the only places in the world where the strange, insect-eating Venus flytrap grows naturally.

Another regional swamp that in the United States occurs only along the southern coasts of Florida is the sub-tropical mangrove swamp. Like salt marshes, which they more or less replace in south Florida, mangrove swamps are flooded each day by tidal water. But being a swamp, the mangrove zone has trees—red mangroves, black mangroves, white mangroves, and buttonwood. These bushy trees are unusual because they can tolerate salty soil and water.

Below *Mangrove swamps are dark and quiet with oozing mud and fingerlike roots.*

Mangrove swamps are dark and quiet. They have "floors" of oozing mud and an understory of exposed, finger-like roots, tangled and rock-hard. Except for raccoon, an occasional snake, and crabs, few animals prowl the web of branches and roots in the mangroves. The mangrove swamp's greatest value is in the tremendous amount of plant litter that it sheds into the coastal environment.

True bogs are wetlands that have an underlayer of **peat**. Peat is the accumulation of decayed plants that slowly builds on the bottom of a lake or pond. Peat can be found in deposits up to 40 feet deep! Many typical bogs

BOGS

develop on the depressions of old lakes that were formed by glaciers. Most bogs can be identified by their layers of peat, the growth of certain evergreen trees and shrubs, and the presence of sphagnum moss.

The vegetation of a bog sometimes grows in a tightly-knit mat and spreads over open water. Walking on the bog mat creates a sensation like walking on a mattress and is the origin of the term "quaking bog."

Bog water usually contains a powerful amount of plant acid. The acid and low oxygen content of bog water prevent many aquatic organisms from living there. Even microscopic bacteria, one of nature's **decomposers**, or decay-causing agents, has a hard time in bogs. In Denmark, a man who had been buried for 2,000 years in a bog was found remarkably well preserved.

With their floating cushions of matted vegetation and tangles of shrubs and sedge, bogs are treacherous places to explore unless they have been "civilized" with a boardwalk. Then visitors can see this curious, floating world rather easily.

None of North America's wetlands is more unique than the Florida Everglades, much of which is protected in

Everglades National Park. The Everglades is neither true marsh nor swamp, yet it has the openness and emergent vegetation of a marsh and pockets of swampy forest. Its pedigree is even more confused because it is connected to a lake—Okeechobee—and it has the water flow of a broad, shallow river. The Seminole Indians called the 'glades Pa Hay-okee, "grassy waters." Author Marjory Stoneman Douglas called them "the river of grass." American soldiers, who tracked into the 'glades in search of fugitive Seminoles in the early 1800s, called them less descriptive names. They found the wet, rock-bottomed 'glades as unyielding a foe as the Seminoles.

The Everglades lie in a shallow basin about 50 miles wide and 100 miles long, stretching from Lake Okeechobee south to Florida Bay. The basin is slightly tilted so that the runoff from Lake Okeechobee during the summer rainy season flows south through the Everglades.

When the Everglades ecosystem is working, the 'glades are a magnificent wetland. The dominant plant is saw-grass, a **sedge** named for its saw-toothed edges. Much of the Everglades appears to be a sea of saw-grass stems, but here and there are islands of trees, locally known as **hammocks**. There are ponds and sloughs, pine forests on "high" ground, and swamp forests of bald cypress and red mangroves. Also in these 'glades are a few of the last Florida panthers, brightly-colored tree snails, wild orchids, a smattering of American crocodiles, bald eagles, ospreys, and dazzling flocks of pink, white, and gray water birds.

MAKING OF THE WETLANDS

Wetlands are wet essentially because they consist of low ground or depressions in the ground that retain water. For various reasons, these are areas where the **water table** is at or above the land's surface. Water table refers to the underground water supply. Rain and snow drain into soil and accumulate in an underground reservoir. When that reservoir rises close to the surface, or above it, a wetland or body of water exists.

Many North American wetlands are products of glaciers. Glaciers are huge rivers of ice. Thousands of years ago they ground across much of Canada and the northern United States. As they slowly retreated northward, they left in their wake scores of imprints in the earth. Many of their depressions retain water in the form of ponds, lakes, bogs, and marshes. The melting of the glaciers helped shape tidal (salt) marshes and river bottom swamps by raising the level of the oceans and, consequently, flooding some rivers over their traditional banks. The action of volcanoes also created some wetland circumstances.

Opposite *A northern bog rimmed by tamarack trees, cattails, and shrubs.*

Reelfoot Lake in Tennessee was formed by volcanic activity.

Many of our bogs and marshes today began as ponds and lakes. Some wetlands show little change over the years, but others change quite dramatically as dead vegetation piles up. When decaying vegetation accumulates, it slowly replaces water in the lake basin. Imagine taking a glass of water and slowly filling it with pennies. Eventually, the mass of the pennies would replace the mass of water. So it is in a lake. The more the lake fills, the shallower its water becomes. Bog plants move in, and what was once clearly a lake now becomes a bog.

Some marshes start life in a similar way. When a shallow pond or river backwater begins to fill with vegetation, it loses its true **aquatic** character and becomes desirable for settlement by marsh life. The marsh, in turn, may become a swamp. As the vegetation replaces water, trees begin to dot the marsh. Some of the sun-loving marsh plants, like sedge, die in the shade of the trees.

The natural process by which one kind of vegetation replaces, or succeeds, another is called **succession**. Succession does not account for the creation of all wetlands. Not all wetlands show evidence of ongoing succession, and some wetlands are created as stream or river courses change or the climate changes. Beavers, too, by damming a stream, can engineer a wetland complex. The pool behind the dam pours into previously dry areas.

Not all wetlands originate from natural causes. People also make wetlands, although the man-made product rarely approaches a natural wetland in its value to wildlife. Dynamite, flood control projects, and road construction work are popular, if often unintentional, means of establishing new wetlands.

PLANTS OF THE WETLANDS

Wetland plants range from the adaptable pink lady's-slipper of dry uplands to highly aquatic plants like water lilies. Since pink lady's-slippers can tolerate a high level of moisture, they have adapted to life in bogs. That ability to tolerate moisture and, in many cases, flooding is the common bond of all wetland plants.

Wetland plants have developed many strategies, or **adaptations**, for living in a wet environment. Spatterdock's leaves float because they have air spaces. Cattails, red mangroves, and several wetland plants produce seeds that float until they contact a suitable site for growth. Some seeds, adapted to flood and drought cycles, can lie **dormant**.

Plants are of great importance to the wetlands. They stabilize the soil. Their leaves and stems are homes for many simple plants and animals—algae and protozoa, for example—that are important food sources for larger animals. Plants conceal invertebrates and fish, provide oxygen for the environment, and represent food, directly or

Opposite *Bald cypress swamps, cool and green, are the haunts of barred owls, pileated woodpeckers, and cottonmouth moccasins.*

24

Above *A dragonfly, one of the wetlands' most colorful insects, pauses on a swamp lily.*

indirectly, for all of the animals in the wetlands.

Common freshwater marsh plants that are rooted are cattails, arrowhead, pickerelweed, and various bullrushes. Other marsh plants float freely or, like water lilies, have long leafstalks on which they send their leaves to the surface. Floating plants include duckweed, water lettuce, and water hyacinth, which has an air-filled leafstalk for buoyancy. Unfortunately, the wetlands would be better off without water hyacinth and its attractive blue flowers. Water hyacinth is an **exotic**, a plant that was not natu-

ally found in the United States. It has caused major problems by clogging waterways.

Northern swamps are dominated by such trees as spruces, white cedar, red maple, yellow birch, black gum, cottonwood, and many others. Loblolly pine, tupelo, ash, and bald cypress are common in southern swamps. Swamps are also among the habitats for blueberries, the brilliant cardinal flower, and skunk cabbage, an early spring wildflower that produces its own heat.

Bogs typically have shrubs such as leatherleaf and poison sumac. The litter

Above *Calopogon orchids can be found in many wetlands throughout much of North America. This one is growing in a Maine bog.*

from poison sumac makes bog water irritating to people's skin. Black spruce, white cedar, and tamarack are typical trees of northern bogs.

The cool, shaded environment of bogs supports some of the most beautiful wildflowers in North America— small yellow lady's-slippers, showy pink lady's-slippers, calopogon orchids, pogonia orchids, and fringed gentians. Some of the strangest plants are there too—the insect-eating pitcher plants, sundew, and butterwort. The insect-eating plants can apparently process the bodies of small insects which they trap

Below *Insect-eating plants, like the sundew, trap insects and eventually convert them into nourishment.*

for nutritional gain. Insect-eating, or carnivorous, plants may have developed their ability to "eat" insects to help compensate for the lack of nutrition available in bog soils.

Along with cypress groves, known as "domes" in south Florida, the Everglades is dotted with clumps of West Indian trees. Because of their subtropical location, the 'glades have been invaded by such West Indian natives as gumbo limbo, paurotis palms, Jamaica dogwood, and Bahama lysilsoma, a favorite tree of Everglades tree snails.

ANIMALS
OF THE WETLANDS

Because wetlands have a wealth of green plants, they have a comparable richness of animal life. The smallest non-microscopic animals are **invertebrates**, animals without backbones. In freshwater wetlands, some of the typical invertebrates are fishing spiders, crawfish, dragonflies, and water striders. In saltwater marshes and mangrove swamps, fiddler crabs and oysters are among the most evident invertebrates.

Coastal wetlands are also the nursery grounds for many species of large saltwater fish. As the fish reach maturity, they leave the wetlands and swim into the open ocean. Freshwater marshes and swamps are habitats for fish that can tolerate warm, shallow, muddy water. These include killifish, mosquitofish, bullheads, and the sunfish clan—largemouth bass, bluegills, pumpkinseeds, and their many cousins.

Since all amphibians lay their eggs in water, wetlands are a favorite gathering place for these soft-skinned animals. Sirens and amphiuma are aquatic amphibians, spending their entire lives in water. Frogs, toads, and salamanders,

Opposite
Anhingas, also known as snakebirds and water turkeys, dry their wings after an underwater hunt.

Right *Alligators live in freshwater wetlands throughout the Southeast.*

Right *Wetlands are a favorite gathering place for the soft-skinned amphibians, such as this bullfrog.*

however, emerge from the water as adults and spend part of their lives on land.

Reptiles are plentiful in the wetlands. Painted turtles and snapping turtles are fond of marshy ponds and swamps. The wood turtle lives in northern swamps and the rare bog turtle of the Northeast is found in bogs. The diamondback terrapin, often associated with brackish water, is found in salt marshes.

Alligators live in freshwater wetlands throughout the Southeast. Their "wallows," or depressions, collect water and sometimes become a last, wet resort for many wetlands animals during drought. The American crocodile is restricted to a few saltwater bays and lagoons of south Florida.

Snakes are common in wetlands. Swamps attract climbing snakes, like the yellow rat snake, as well as swimming snakes. The cottonmouth, water snakes, mud snakes, and swamp snakes are typical wetlands varieties.

Wetlands are attractive to over 200 species of North American birds, although each species may use the wetlands for some purpose other than nesting. Warblers, for example, of many species flit among the swamp's canopy of leaves and branches. Other warblers, like the yellowthroat, nest in the wetlands. Yellow-headed blackbirds, redwing blackbirds, and boat-tailed grackles are also typical perching birds that nest in marsh vegetation.

Among the larger birds in the wetlands are many of our most beautiful water birds, including the long-legged cranes, herons, egrets, ibises, roseate spoonbills, and wood storks. All of them nest in wetlands of one type or another.

While wading birds prowl the edges of pools or wade into relatively shallow water, other water birds can be seen floating, at least momentarily, on the open water. Several of these birds—grebes, anhingas, cormorants, and many ducks—dive for their food. Coots, geese, swans, and the so-called "puddle ducks" bob for their food or snap up edibles from the surface. The long necks of swans help them reach plants that other shallow feeders cannot.

Forster's tern, the black tern, California gulls, and Franklin's gulls are associated with western marshes. Gulls are very adaptable birds. They can pluck food from the water's surface or from the water's edge. They also feed far from the marshes, and flocks of Franklin's gulls were given credit in the 1800s for stemming a plague of grasshoppers in Utah. The sharp-billed terns, although related to gulls, are not nearly as adaptable. They snatch fish from the surface of open water.

Rails are common in marshes, but they are very difficult to see. Secretive birds, rails hide, feed, and nest among the stalks of marsh plants. The short-eared owl, northern harrier, and barred owl hunt small animals in the wetlands. White pelicans fly to broad marshes to

Left Striking, black-capped Franklin's gulls nest in Western marshes.

Left Marshes are havens for great numbers of waterfowl—ducks, geese, and swans. Blue-wing teal shown here.

herd fish within easy reach of their dip-net pouches.

With the exception of the anhinga, which sinks to swim, the swimming birds of wetlands have oily, water-proofed feathers. Most of them also have webbed feet to assist swimming and diving. The purple gallinule and moorhen, however, have long toes with discs on them. That arrangement helps these birds step onto the broad leaves of floating aquatic plants and hunt where other birds cannot.

The beaks of wetlands birds help demonstrate each species' particular adaptation to a special **niche**, or place, within the total wetland environment. Shoveler ducks and roseate spoonbills strain water with comblike strainers in their bills. Ibis use down-curved bills to probe the mud. Herons, egrets, and the anhinga all have daggerlike beaks for spearing. The wood stork has a fairly blunt, slightly down-curved bill. The wood stork drags its lower bill as it stalks along a shore. When the bill touches a small fish, it reflexively snaps together with the upper bill, catching the prey between.

The variety of bills forces the birds to be specialized in what they hunt and where they hunt it. Herons and egrets

Below *A sunfish falls prey to a river otter, a larger relative of another wetlands hunter, the mink.*

have a similar bill structure, but nature has avoided conflict by making the birds in many different sizes. Long-legged great blue herons and great egrets can hunt in much deeper water than little blue herons or snowy egrets. Green herons avoid any suggestion of competition with their cousins by hunting from overhanging tree limbs.

Many mammals—deer, moose, black bears, raccoons, snowshoe hares—come to the wetlands to drink or feed. The marsh rats, bog lemmings, marsh and swamp rabbits, otter, muskrat, mink, beaver, and nutria, an exotic from South America, are wetlands residents. Many of them have waterproofed fur and webbed feet, useful adaptations for wetland life.

Below *Raccoons visit wetlands for a wide variety of foods, including oysters, crawfish, and frogs.*

6 THE FLOW OF ENERGY

Plants and animals in the wetlands are constantly working to manufacture or consume food. Food provides the energy needed to function. The flow of energy from one life form to another isn't always obvious to an observer, but it is always taking place.

Plants manufacture their own food. They are called **producers** because they can convert sunlight and nutrients from air, water, and soil into food. This food-producing process is called **photosyn-thesis**. In one way or another, animals in the wetland have to tap into the food resources manufactured and stored by plants.

Some of the wetland invertebrates eat living green plants, thus unlocking for themselves the food and energy stored in plant tissues. More animals, however, feed on **detritus**. Detritus includes edible particles of food which are produced when stems, leaves, and twigs have been partially decayed. But whether the invertebrates, or the larger vertebrates, are eating plants directly or plant detritus, they are eating plant material.

Opposite Energy flows from small consumer to a larger consumer when little blue heron gobbles a lizard from coastal wetland.

All animals are **consumers** because they eat, or consume, food rather than produce it. The invertebrates become prey for larger animals. Yet even when a mink kills and eats a muskrat, the mink is indirectly taking its energy from plants. After all, the muskrat grew by munching on cattails and other wetland plants. The muskrat gained energy from the plant and the mink gained some of the same energy from the muskrat.

The sequence of energy exchange from sunlight to cattail, cattail to muskrat, and muskrat to mink is called a **food chain**. Another familiar food chain of the wetlands begins with mosquito larvae, which live on microscopic organisms in the water. Some mosquito larvae are eaten by mosquitofish. The little mosquitofish, in turn, may be gobbled by a heron or a larger fish, animals near the "top" of the food chains.

Many of the wetland food chains are much more complex. In their entirety, the food chains of any wetland would show hundreds of exchanges of energy. They would include organisms from microscopic bacteria to the community's largest trees and animals. The chains would interconnect and the result would be a giant web of plant and animal interdependence; the web would show that the plants and animals in the community depend upon each other.

Among the animals in the wetlands are the plant-eaters (**herbivores**), meat-eaters (**carnivores**), and the plant and animal-eaters (**omnivores**). The ability of the wetland **ecosystem** to function without damage to itself is based upon the successful exchange of energy between plants and groups of consuming animals. Part of the success of the system depends on each plant and animal having a niche that doesn't normally interfere with another niche. Two herbivores, for instance, who live in the same specialized wetland habitat, won't necessarily eat the same plant. While the muskrat consumes large, green plants, other herbivores, such as certain insects, eat tiny strands of algae. The mink tends to hunt along the wetland's edges. Its cousin, the otter, hunts in the water. Neither animal's place, or niche, in the wetlands contends with the other's.

The ecosystem begins to break down if it is interfered with. If all the mink are trapped from a wetland, for example, the muskrat population might explode. Too many muskrats would reduce the population of green plants. Soon the muskrats would actually eat themselves into starvation by eliminating their food source. For awhile at least, the wetland would be lacking in mink, muskrats, and a healthy population of green plants.

If taking away from the ecosystem is harmful, so too can be adding to it. In Florida, the introduction of numerous exotic plants and animals has damaged the wetlands by upsetting the balance of native plants and animals. The water hyacinth, introduced from South America, has grown splendidly in Florida. By spreading over water surfaces it has, among other things, taken over the niche of some native plants and blocked sunlight from aquatic organisms.

CONSERVATION OF THE WETLANDS

The introduction of exotics is only one of the problems that the North American wetlands have endured. It isn't easy to make a wetland dry, but North Americans have been quite successful at the task. The business of making wetlands dry—"reclaiming" them— has been going on since the first Europeans arrived in the New World. In the twentieth century, the practice has intensified.

Wetlands are usually drained, or altered in some way, to create more land for agricultural use. The same marsh that produces cattails and ducks, or sawgrass and herons, will also pro-

Below *Fahka-hatchee State Reserve, part of the Big Cypress Swamp in Florida, is a showplace of wetlands vegetation.*

duce corn and soybeans, or lettuce and watermelons, if it can be rid of its water. The muck of marsh and swamp bottoms is certainly fertile soil.

Coastal wetlands have been drained or dumped in largely for use by industry or land developers. Cities by the seas have grown enormously in recent decades.

Precise figures do not exist, but millions of acres of North American wetlands have been drained in the past 100 years. Fortunately, attitudes toward destroying wetlands have changed in recent years. The soggy, sloppy places that once made people cringe and shiver are now being recognized as extremely useful and valuable.

Wetlands are important to people as well as to wildlife. They help control flooding because they are natural water storage basins. They filter many kinds of pollutants and they help stabilize our own environment through the release of oxygen by wetlands plants. Wetlands add water to the underground water tables from which much of our drinking water comes. Along sea coasts, wetlands help prevent erosion from tidal forces.

Despite their tremendous importance to people and animals, wetlands were being destroyed like so many mosquitoes. California destroyed nearly 90 percent of its wetlands. Connecticut buried nearly half of its tidal marshes. Iowa drained 99 percent of its natural marshes. Illinois drained 90 percent of its natural marshland. The Everglades of Florida have been lanced with canals and altered by water control devices. The state of Florida and the federal government are having to spend millions of dollars to try and undo some of the damage and save Everglades National Park. Between the middle 1950s and 1980, 9.2 million acres of wetlands in the United States alone were ruined.

The destruction of wetlands has not stopped, but the pace of destruction has slowed. Efforts are even underway in some states to restore historical wetlands that have been reclaimed. Government officials have become much more alert to the value of wetlands and, for the most part, are no longer encouraging their wholesale destruction.

Wetlands are one of our most interesting and valuable resources. Protecting them from chemical pollution, dumping, ditching, and draining is not a simple business. But protecting them is a wise investment for all of us.

GLOSSARY

adaptation   a characteristic of function, form, or behavior that improves an organism's survival chances in a particular habitat

aquatic   of or referring to water

brackish   referring to a mixture of both fresh- and saltwater

bromeliad   a specific group of subtropical and tropical epiphytes or air plants

carnivore   referring to an animal that eats meat

consumer   an animal, so named because it must eat, or consume, to live

decomposer   an organism, most often bacteria and fungi, that consumes dead tissue and reduces it to small particles

detritus   tiny particles of decaying remains of plants and animals

dormant   a state of inactivity due to the slowing or stopping of normal functions

ecosystem   a system of exchanges of food and energy between plants and animals and their environment

emergent   a plant that grows with its stem partially exposed and partially submerged

epiphyte   a plant that grows on another plant and gathers its nourishment from air and rain; an air plant

exotic   a plant or animal introduced into an environment in which it did not naturally occur

food chain   the transfer of energy from green plants through a series of consuming animals

glacier   a massive river of ice that forms on high ground when snowfall exceeds summer melting

habitat   an animal's or plant's immediate surroundings; its specific place within the community

hammock   a grove of trees standing more or less apart from the surrounding land or water, particularly in Florida

herbivore   plant-eating animal

invertebrate   an animal without a backbone

niche   an organism's role or job in the community

omnivore   an animal with the capability to eat both plant and animal material

organism   a living being

peat   layers of partly decayed plant material characterized by high acid content and low oxygen

photosynthesis   the process by which green plants produce simple food sugars through the use of sunlight and chlorophyll

pocosin   a type of shrubby swamp of the southeastern United States

producer   a green plant, so named for its ability to manufacture, or produce, food

sedge   a long-stemmed, grass-like plant usually with solid triangular stems

succession   the gradual replacement of one plant community by another

water table   the level of the water stored underground

WETLANDS SITES

The following is a sampling of outstanding sites where you can expect to find characteristic plants and animals of the wetlands and outstanding scenery:

CANADA

Manitoba
The Delta Marsh, Portage la Prairie, Manitoba
Northwest Territories
Wood Buffalo National Park, Fort Smith, Northwest Territories
Saskatchewan
Grasslands National Park, Val Marie, Saskatchewan

UNITED STATES

Alaska
Kenai National Moose Range, Kenai, Alaska
California
Tule Lake, Lower Klamath, and Sacramento National Wildlife Refuges, Tule Lake, California
Florida
Ding Darling National Wildlife Refuge, Sanibel, Florida
Everglades National Park, Homestead, Florida
Maine
Acadia National Park, Bar Harbor, Maine
Maryland
Blackwater National Wildlife Refuge, Cambridge, Maryland
Massachusetts
Cape Cod National Seashore, Eastham, Massachusetts
Michigan
Isle Royale National Park, Houghton, Michigan
Oregon
Upper Klamath National Wildlife Refuge, Klamath, Oregon
Texas
Aransas National Wildlife Refuge, Austwell, Texas
Utah
Bear River Migratory Bird Refuge, Brigham City, Utah

ACTIVITIES

Here are some activities and projects that will help you learn more about the North American wetlands:

1. Make observations of plants and animals in a wetland near your home. Use a notebook, sketchpad, or camera to help you be a careful observer. Later, use a library to find out more about some of the plants and animals you have seen or heard. Find out how each has special characteristics that enable it to live in a wetlands environment.

2. Draw a food chain or several food chains of a particular wetlands environment, such as a salt marsh. Show in your drawings the relationships of sunlight to plants, plants to animals, and animals to animals.

3. Draw one of the typical wetlands animals. Explain below your drawing which of the animal's structural characteristics (webbed feet on a duck, for example) make it especially suited for a wetlands environment.

4. Create a collage of wetlands plants and animals.

5. Join a conservation organization that promotes wetlands protection and restoration. Several national and international organizations are listed here:

UNITED STATES
National Wildlife Federation
1412 Sixteenth St., NW
Washington, DC 20036

The Nature Conservancy
1800 N. Kent St.
Arlington, VA 22209

CANADA
Canadian Nature Federation
75 Albert St., Suite 203
Ottawa, Ontario K1P 9Z9

The Young Naturalist Foundation
59 Front St. E.
Toronto, Ontario M5E 1B3

47

INDEX

Numbers in boldface type refer to photo pages.